Great Artists
Pablo Picasso

ABDO
Publishing Company

Adam G. Klein

visit us at
www.abdopublishing.com

Published by ABDO Publishing Company, 4940 Viking Drive, Edina, Minnesota 55435.
Copyright © 2007 by Abdo Consulting Group, Inc. International copyrights reserved in all
countries. No part of this book may be reproduced in any form without written permission from
the publisher. The Checkerboard Library™ is a trademark and logo of ABDO Publishing
Company.

Printed in the United States.

Cover Photo: Getty Images
Interior Photos: Art Resource pp. 9, 15, 25, 27; Bridgeman Art Library pp. 11, 13, 19, 23; Corbis
        pp. 8, 22; Getty Images pp. 1, 5, 16, 17, 21, 27, 29

Pablo Picasso art images pp. 5, 9, 11, 13, 15, 16, 19, 21, 23, 25, 27, 29 © 2005 Estate of
        Pablo Picasso / Artists Rights Society (ARS), New York.

Series Coordinator: Megan M. Gunderson
Editors: Rochelle Baltzer, Megan M. Gunderson
Cover Design: Neil Klinepier
Interior Design: Dave Bullen

Library of Congress Cataloging-in-Publication Data

Klein, Adam G., 1976-
 Pablo Picasso / Adam G. Klein.
     p. cm. -- (Great artists)
 Includes index.
 ISBN-10 1-59679-733-9
 ISBN-13 978-1-59679-733-8
 1. Picasso, Pablo, 1881-1973--Juvenile literature. 2. Artists--France--Biography--Juvenile
literature. I. Picasso, Pablo, 1881-1973. II. Title III. Series: Klein, Adam G., 1976- . Great
artists.

 N6853.P5K43 2006
 709'.2--dc22
                                                                    2005017891

Contents

Pablo Picasso

Pablo Picasso was born an artist. Even at a young age, he had a promising future. He always had lofty goals and reached for success. But even he could never have guessed the great influence he would have on the world of art.

Picasso's artwork, especially his paintings, is considered some of the greatest of all time. Picasso, along with Georges Braque, is considered the inventor of the modern art movement Cubism. Rarely did he slow down in his work, even though he was an artist for more than 80 years!

Picasso often changed his artistic style. As soon as he learned how to create artwork in one style, he moved on to the next. He didn't like to return to his past works. Instead, Picasso always looked for something new. He searched for different ways to express himself.

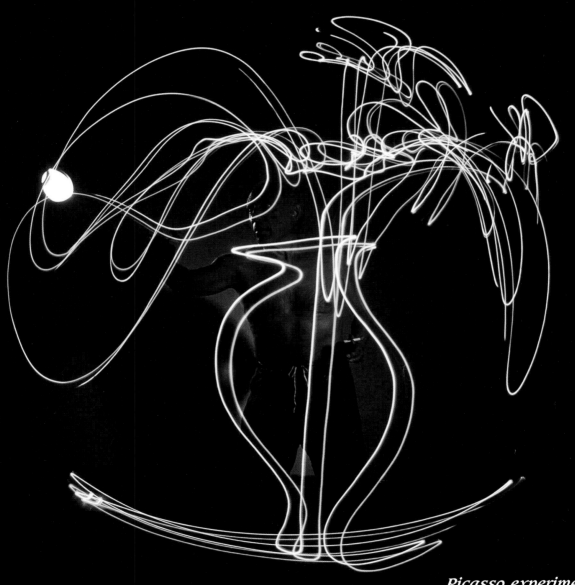

Picasso experimented with photography, which allowed him to "paint" with light.

Timeline

1881 ~ On October 25, Pablo Ruiz y Picasso was born in Málaga, Spain.

1897 ~ Picasso won awards for *Science and Charity*.

1900 ~ Picasso had an exhibition at Els Quatre Gats; his work was included in the Paris Universal Exhibition; he completed *Le Moulin de la Galette*.

1901 ~ Carles Casagemas died on February 17; Picasso's Blue Period began.

1904 ~ Picasso's Rose Period began.

1905 ~ Picasso completed *The Saltimbanques*.

1907 ~ Picasso completed *Les Demoiselles d'Avignon*.

1917 ~ Picasso began creating set designs and costumes for ballets.

1925 ~ On February 14, Picasso participated in the first Surrealist exhibition in Paris, France; Picasso painted *The Dance*.

1937 ~ Picasso painted *Guernica*.

1963 ~ The Picasso Museum opened in Barcelona, Spain.

1973 ~ Picasso died on April 8.

Fun Facts

- When he was young, family members would ask Pablo Picasso to create artwork for them. Besides drawing, he cut animals and other shapes out of paper. Sometimes, he used them to create shadows on the wall.

- In the beginning, Picasso signed his paintings "Pablo Ruiz Picasso." By 1901, he had stopped using "Ruiz."

- Sometimes, artists paint over an older work with a newer one. Picasso's *Last Moments* was found underneath *La Vie*. Picasso exhibited *Last Moments* in 1900 at the Paris Universal Exhibition. He painted *La Vie* just a few years later.

- After a visit in 1934, Picasso never returned to Spain. But, he always remained loyal to his home country.

Pablo Ruiz y Picasso was born on October 25, 1881, in Málaga, Spain. His father, José Ruiz Blasco, worked as a professor of drawing. His mother was named Maria Picasso López. She worked hard to raise their three children.

Pablo began drawing at a very young age. Before he was old enough to talk, he would simply draw the things he wanted to have. Some even say his first word was "pencil."

His father's experience, encouragement, and training helped Pablo during these early years. One of Pablo's earliest paintings, *Picador*, is from around 1889.

Picadors often perform on horseback during bullfights. They wear special costumes that include low, broad-brimmed hats and short, decorated jackets.

He already showed promising talent with this bullfighting scene. In 1891, the family moved to La Coruña. This city is on the northwest coast of Spain. Pablo had his first exhibition there at the age of 13.

Picasso most likely painted Picador *after seeing a bullfight in Málaga with his father.*

School Days

By September 1895, Pablo's father had a job offer to teach in Barcelona, Spain. There at La Llotja, or the Barcelona School of Fine Arts, Pablo continued studying art.

Later in life, Pablo said he had been given one month to complete the La Llotja entrance exam. He claimed that because he was so talented, he returned the next day with his exam complete. This story was not true. Still, the school officials were impressed by the young artist's skills and accepted Pablo for classes.

At school, Pablo's art continued to improve. In 1897, he won a gold medal at the Málaga Provincial Exhibition for his painting *Science and Charity*. He also received an honorable mention at the Fine Arts Exhibition in Madrid, Spain. Also in 1897, Pablo attended the Royal Academy of San Fernando in Barcelona. But later that year, he left the academy for Madrid.

However, Pablo soon returned to Barcelona. There, he began designing menus and posters for Els Quatre Gats, or "The Four Cats." This was a popular gathering place for artists.

Pablo was always experimenting with different forms of art. For his projects at Els Quatre Gats, he was influenced by the work of Henri de Toulouse-Lautrec. The menus and posters were a hit. And in February 1900, Els Quatre Gats held an exhibition of 150 of Pablo's various works.

Picasso modeled the doctor in **Science** *and* **Charity** *after his father. José represents science, while the nun represents charity.*

Blue and Rose

In Barcelona, Picasso shared a studio with Carles Casagemas. In 1900, they traveled to Paris, France. Picasso had been asked to exhibit an example of his work at the Paris Universal Exhibition. *Last Moments* was chosen to represent Spain.

Picasso continued to grow as an artist in Paris. That same year, he completed *Le Moulin de la Galette*. It was his first Parisian painting. Then, he returned to Spain.

Picasso was enjoying his success. But his life changed on February 17, 1901, when Casagemas died. Picasso became depressed. He withdrew from his friends, and his art changed dramatically.

Picasso started to paint mostly in the color blue, which reflected his sadness. Many of these Blue Period paintings deal directly with the death of Casagemas. And in general, the subjects of Picasso's Blue Period paintings have a look of sadness to them. This includes the man in *The Old Guitarist*, which Picasso completed in 1903.

Toulouse-Lautrec and Pierre-Auguste Renoir influenced Picasso's early work. All three artists painted the Moulin de la Galette. This is Picasso's impression of the popular dance hall.

In 1904, Picasso returned to Paris and began his Rose Period. He soon made new friends and even found a girlfriend, Fernande Olivier. His rose-colored works were filled with happier images. Picasso finished *The Saltimbanques* in 1905. Like many Rose Period paintings, the subjects of this work are circus performers.

Cubism

Picasso's style was continuing to **evolve**. As always, he wanted to create something new and different. In summer 1906, Picasso and Olivier moved to Gósol, Spain. Picasso found the solitude of this small mountain village inspiring.

Around this time, Picasso grew fond of African art. He wanted to combine its look with his own. Picasso decided that the world of art needed something different. He thought images could be presented in a more pure form. So, Picasso got to work on his new ideas.

One of Picasso's earliest experiments with this new form was *Les Demoiselles d'Avignon*. He completed this work in 1907. People called the new style Cubism because of the boxlike images in the paintings.

At first, most people were not impressed with this new style. Still, Picasso and fellow artist Georges Braque thought it was worth experimenting with the idea. They removed their figures from settings and broke them down into basic shapes. Eventually, they made their images appear flat.

Artist's Corner

Pablo Picasso

In 1908, a critic described Braque's painting *Houses at L'Estaques* as being made of cubes. He did not mean the statement as a compliment. But, Braque was not discouraged. Soon, the Cubist movement caught on.

Cubism emphasizes basic shapes by using outlines without much interior detail. The artists unfolded their flattened images to show different sides of an object at the same time. Some Cubist paintings simply have more angular lines. Others, such as *Man with a Guitar*, are basically composed of simple shapes.

Early Cubist paintings have depth through the careful use of a variety of colors. Later, Cubists used similar colors in one painting. This helps the viewer focus on just the structure of the figure.

Works such as *Man with a Guitar* can seem abstract, or unclear, at first glance. But because Picasso was a talented Cubist painter, the basic forms of a face and a guitar remain visible. They are simply broken down into pure elements such as color and shape.

Picasso painted **Man with a Guitar** *in 1911.*

Parade

Picasso worked with Cubism in many forms. He wanted his work to be recognizable while providing the least amount of information possible. By 1912, he had experimented with Cubist sculpture. That year, Picasso assembled *Guitar* out of sheet metal.

Around the same time, Olivier left Picasso. Then, Picasso fell in love with a woman named Eva Gouel. Unfortunately, Gouel suffered from **tuberculosis**. She tried to hide her sickness for years, but eventually she had to stay in a hospital. Picasso remained with Gouel until her death on December 14, 1915.

Eventually, Picasso felt that his artwork needed to change again. He returned to creating realistic drawings while he waited for his next big opportunity. Picasso got his

In 2001, this portrait of Olga Kokhlova failed to sell at auction.

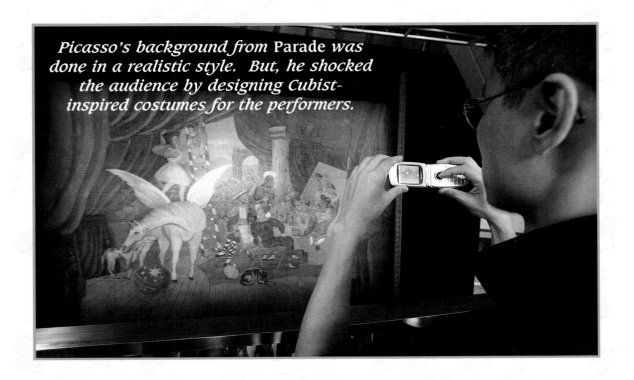
Picasso's background from Parade *was done in a realistic style. But, he shocked the audience by designing Cubist-inspired costumes for the performers.*

chance in 1917. Sergey Diaghilev was directing the Ballets Russes production of *Parade*. Picasso was asked to create costumes and design a set for the ballet.

Picasso rushed off to Rome, Italy, to work on the design. The ballet was a great opportunity for Picasso because he was always interested in the performing arts. While working on the project, Picasso met a dancer named Olga Kokhlova. They fell in love.

Fame and Fortune

On July 12, 1918, Picasso married Kokhlova. Over the next few years, Picasso continued working on various ballets. So, he spent a lot of time away from home.

Picasso's first son, Paulo, was born on February 4, 1921. The same year, the first book about Picasso was published. By this time, Picasso claimed to be earning 1.5 million francs per year. This was about $280,000 a year.

To stay interested in his work, Picasso continued to change his **techniques** and themes. And, he worked in many different artistic styles at once. Picasso often combined styles from many countries, including Spain, France, and Italy. In the 1920s, he added new themes such as motherhood. And for the ballet *Mercure*, his work became less boxlike.

The Surrealists applauded Picasso's design work for **Mercure.** *It was Picasso's last ballet.*

Picasso's fame grew. His exhibits started to be shown across Europe. And, more articles about him appeared in magazines. Members of the art world began to notice his work, too. Soon, a group of artists wanted to recruit Picasso to join a new art movement called Surrealism.

The Surrealist

Picasso met André Breton in 1923. Breton helped start the Surrealist movement. Surrealism was based on dreams and how the mind works. Picasso never called himself a Surrealist, but the new style suited him. He joined the first Surrealist exhibition in Paris. It began on November 14, 1925, at the Galerie Pierre.

That same year, Picasso painted *The Dance*. Some people think this early Surrealist work reflects his life at that time. He was beginning to drift away from his wife. In many of his paintings, Picasso's subjects became more and more **distorted** as Picasso showed the negative side of his life.

Art dealer Ambroise Vollard soon **commissioned** Picasso. From 1930 to 1937, Picasso created a series of mythological **etchings** for him.

Picasso and Kokhlova separated in the early 1930s. Soon after, Picasso started seeing model Marie-Thérèse Walter. They

had a daughter named Maya. They moved to Boisgeloup, France, where Picasso had bought a house. There, he worked on sculpture. Picasso's world was changing fast, and trouble was coming soon.

In 1935, Picasso posed with one of his realistic paintings of Kokhlova. She had said she wanted to be able to recognize her face.

During the 1930s, tensions were rising throughout Europe. Countries were fighting each other, and people were turning against their governments. In July 1936, **fascists** supported by General Francisco Franco started the **Spanish Civil War**.

At this time, the Spanish government **commissioned** Picasso to create a work of art for the 1937 Paris World's Fair. Picasso was provided with a large studio in Paris. But at first, he did not know what to paint.

On April 26, 1937, German **allies** of Franco destroyed the town of Guernica in northern Spain. More than 1,600 people were killed. Picasso sometimes painted political works to express his own views. When Picasso heard about this tragedy, he felt compelled to paint it.

Soldiers walk through the destruction left after the bombing of Guernica.

When Picasso painted Guernica, *his artistic style was still evolving. His figures were more curvy and less boxy than his earlier Cubist works.*

Picasso completed *Guernica* in just three weeks. The large black-and-white painting shows images of people suffering. Many people did not like the painting at first, but **critics** praised it. Soon, people understood Picasso's message. *Guernica* traveled across the world as a symbol of what war could do to ordinary people.

Promoting Peace

During **World War II**, Picasso stayed in Europe. There, he continued creating and exhibiting his sculptures and drawings. Still, he was always looking for a new challenge.

In summer 1946, Picasso's friend Georges Ramié invited him to see his pottery workshop. So Picasso went to Vallauris, France. Over the next couple years, Picasso enjoyed figuring out different ways to shape his **ceramic** objects.

Meanwhile, Picasso had been with his new love, Françoise Gilot. They had a son, Claude, in 1947. Their daughter, Paloma, was born in 1949.

During this time, Picasso actively promoted peace. He attended several peace conferences. In August 1948, he went to the Congress of Intellectuals for Peace in Poland. His drawing of a dove, *La Colombe*, was used to promote peace. It appeared on the poster for the Congress of Peace, held in Paris in February 1949.

Doves are a symbol of peace. Over the years, Picasso used doves in drawings, paintings, and ceramic designs.

Painting Series

As Picasso grew older, people were amazed at his good health. He was physically strong his whole life. And, he had the energy to work at astonishing speeds. Throughout the 1960s, Picasso created several series of paintings. He based the series on various other artists, their models, and their **techniques**.

In 1963, the Picasso Museum opened in Barcelona, Spain. Picasso had not lived in Barcelona for a long time. Still, he created a place where his masterpieces could be displayed after he was gone. Today, there are more than 3,500 works by Picasso in the museum's permanent collection.

Picasso enjoyed his popularity. He remained in contact with a few friends. But, Picasso often felt he was wasting time when he was with friends and family rather than painting. By the late 1960s, Picasso decided to return to creating **etchings** rather than series paintings.

Studying the Masters

In the 1950s, Picasso began studying the works of the old masters. The old masters are the talented artists who had come before him. Picasso took classic paintings of varying styles and redid them in his own way.

In 1955, Picasso created 15 paintings based on a work by Eugène Delacroix called Femmes d'Alger. And, he reworked paintings by the Realist Jean Courbet and the Impressionist Édouard Manet.

Picasso also studied the work of El Greco, who painted in the late 1500s and early 1600s. Picasso painted Portrait of an Artist, after El Greco (right), based on an El Greco portrait (left). The main elements of El Greco's work remain. These include the large white collar and the contrast between the pale face and dark clothing. However, Picasso recreated the work in his own style.

Etchings

In 1966, there was a large exhibit of Picasso's work in Paris to celebrate his 85th birthday. Picasso did not care to attend. So, he avoided the exhibit.

From May to September 1968, Picasso created a group of more than 300 **etchings**. From 1971 to 1972, he created another extensive set of etchings.

Picasso's health began to fail, but it did not slow down his work. Picasso did not want to let his age get in the way of his life. However, Picasso died on April 8, 1973, after suffering from lung congestion. A bronze sculpture was placed on his grave. It was made from an **engraving** he had drawn 50 years earlier, called *La femme au vase*.

By some counts, Picasso created up to 50,000 works of art during his lifetime. His career took him from living in nearly starving conditions, to living as a master artist.

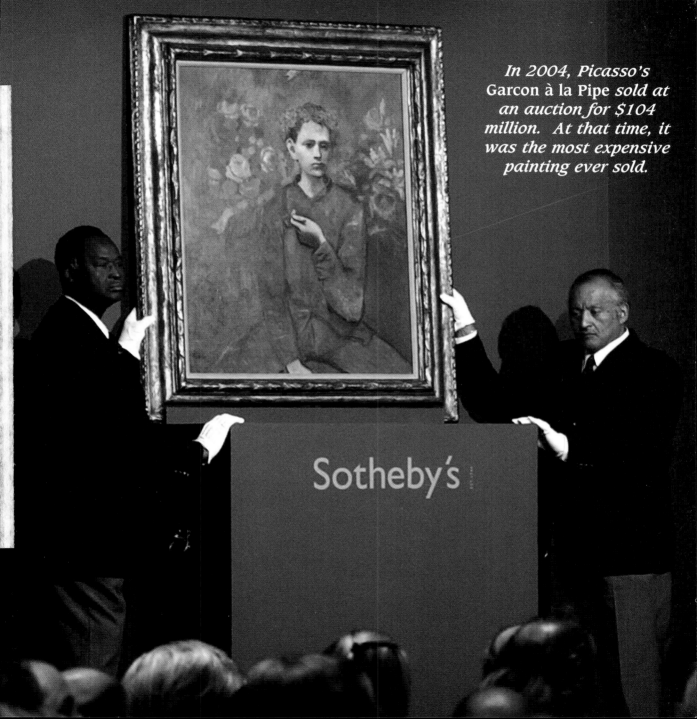

In 2004, Picasso's Garcon à la Pipe *sold at an auction for $104 million. At that time, it was the most expensive painting ever sold.*

Glossary

allies - people or countries that agree to help each other in times of need.

ceramic - of or relating to a nonmetallic product, such as pottery or porcelain.

commission - a request to complete a work, such as a painting, for a certain person. To be commissioned is to be given such a request.

critic - a professional who gives his or her opinion on art or performances.

distort - to twist something out of its normal shape or condition.

engraving - a print, usually made by cutting designs into wood or metal.

etching - a picture or design, usually made by printing an image that was created by scarring the surface of a material.

evolve - to develop gradually.

fascism - a political philosophy that favors a dictatorship and places nation or race above individual rights.

Spanish Civil War - from 1936 to 1939, fought in Spain. The Nationalist forces overthrew the Republican government.

technique - a method or style in which something is done.

tuberculosis - a disease that affects the lungs.

World War II - from 1939 to 1945, fought in Europe, Asia, and Africa. Great Britain, France, the United States, the Soviet Union, and their allies were on one side. Germany, Italy, Japan, and their allies were on the other side.

Saying It

Ambroise Vollard - ahn-brwawz vaw-lawr
Georges Braque - zhawrzh brawk
Henri de Toulouse-Lautrec - ahn-ree duh too-looz-loh-trehk
Málaga - MAH-lah-guh
Sergey Diaghilev - syihr-GYAY DYAWG-yihl-yihf
tuberculosis - tu-buhr-kyuh-LOH-suhs

Web Sites

To learn more about Pablo Picasso, visit ABDO Publishing Company on the World Wide Web at **www.abdopub.com**. Web sites about Picasso are featured on our Book Links page. These links are routinely monitored and updated to provide the most current information available.

Index